Write that Book!
You Have a Book in You! Now Write it!

Edie Bayer

ISBN: 0692350756
ISBN-13: 978-0692350751

For Help and Assistance, contact:
Kingdom Promoters
www.KingdomPromoters.org
Edie@KingdomPromoters.org

DEDICATION

This book is dedicated to the Author within all of us.

CONTENTS

ACKNOWLEDGMENTS

Thank you to my husband
Thank you to my high school English Teacher
Thank you to Cliff, who taught me to read the dictionary like a book

Thank you to Jesus, who is my light

Preface

You have a book in you! Now write it!

So, you want to write a book! Congratulations! You have joined the ranks of 81% of all Americans.

Of course, the question is now, not do you WANT to write and publish your book --- but HOW?

Once people found out I had written multiple books, so many of them asked me how to get their own book published....Where to find time....How do I do it?

This book is written with those answers in mind, and a whole lot more. Keep reading, to find out not just HOW to write your book, but how to market it as well!

Edie Bayer

2

1. YOU HAVE A BOOK IN YOU!
NOW WRITE IT!

"You have a book in you! Now write it!"

This phrase first came out of my mouth in December 2011.

At that time I was writing my very first book, *Spritual Espionage -- Going Undercover for the Kingdom of God!* During the creation of this book, the Lord sent me to a Presbyterian Church on a spiritual mission. I had a run-in, or more accurately, a 'run-into', the hospice chaplain that was giving the message that Sunday. In his sermon, this minister told story after story about people who he had cared for – and about – that had died while under his spiritual care in hospice.

As I tried to bolt out the door after service, he stopped me in the doorway, which is when I literally ran into him for the second time that day.

As he started excitedly shaking my hand, I was overcome by a prophetic spirit and told him, rather boldly as I recall, "You are an author!" He humbly shook his head 'No', but I poked him in the chest, and said, "Yes, you are! You have a book in you --- Now Write it!"

That very same statement applies to you, the reader of this book. I am poking you in the chest right now, telling you, **"YOU ARE AN AUTHOR! You have a book in you --- Now Write it!"**

Let's face it. If you didn't think you had something to say you would never have picked up this book! You are called to write! This book is a magnet for you. In fact, all books are magnets for you! Probably, like me, as you read book after book you tell yourself, "I can do that! I can write like that!"

Well, the truth is, YOU CAN. All you need to do is **DO IT**.

But how?

The purpose of this book is to answer that question and demystify the process to help you **DO IT**. This book lays out in the simplest of terms exactly how to get your book out of your heart and your head, onto the pages of your word processing program and into print.

So, one more time – **You are an AUTHOR! You have a book in you – Now WRITE IT!**

Ready? Let's do this.

2. STEP ONE – THE IDEA

Where does the idea for your book come from? For me, all ideas come from God. He uses incredible sources to inspire mankind, whether we acknowledge Him or not. Nature. Weather. Sound. Emotions. Scripture. Relationship. All of these have been inspiration for Man, blessings from God, and foundations for literature from antiquity, and I am sure, for all of eternity.

For me, all of the ideas for all of my books began in God. Not just the first or second book, but all of them, including this one, and the next one, and the one after that I'm sure! They're ALL His ideas.

God gives me so MANY ideas, and I am sure He gives you

many, many ideas as well.

But out of all of the ideas that have presented themselves to you, which of them do you actually put pen to paper?

Well, this is what happened for me, and out of that came a sort of "formula" for making it happen.

As I mentioned at the outset, for my very first book, God sent me on a mission to take back territory that the enemy had stolen. The entire journey is chronicled in my first book, *Spiritual Espionage --- Going Undercover for the Kingdom of God!*

(Note – it is VERY satisfying to be able to use "My FIRST Book..." in a sentence! It is even more fulfilling to say, "My Second Book..." and "My Fourth Book..." Just wait! You'll be thrilled too!)

This book started out as a humble journal, but as I was journaling this series of events, I realized that God wanted me to make it into a book. I had always WANTED to write a book, so He merely gave me the vehicle....a series of assignments that He instructed me to journal. When I started to put the book together, I simply used each church that I visited as a chapter.

God wanted me to write the book, that much is clear. The "surprise ending" even surprised me!

But I know it was much more than that. When a year had gone by since I had completed the book save for final editing and printing, the Lord spoke to me as I was setting up the book table for Darren Canning, our prophet friend who was ministering at our house. The Lord said to me, "Your book should be on this table!"

That did it. I set out to finish up the book and get it into print, and I did. It took two years start to finish, but finished it was. I was never so excited in my life as I was to see that first copy of that book!

However, for me, the most mind-boggling part was that the Lord had already started me on a second book, even before the first one was completely done! That is another story entirely, explained in the preface of my second book, *Power Thieves – Seven Spirits that Steal Your Power and How to Get it Back!* This book teaches how to win the spiritual war against seven of the most common spirits that steal your God-given power.

It's very interesting how the Lord gave me the idea for the second book. He told me to grab a pencil and some paper, and just write down what I heard him say. The first thing was Jezebel, then the past, then pride, rebellion, submission, judgmental, disobedience. He explained that these were the chapters of the second book. I never thought anything of it, I just sat down to write.

I was several chapters into writing it before I realized that this list of spirits' names had already been given to me...in the *last chapter of my first book*! You can read it for yourself. At the very end of the first book the Lord listed spirits that He wants to free His children -- including you and me.

The third book, *Spiritual Lightning Rods, Connected to the Father of Lights* was actually my **FIRST** book. See, years before it ever came into being, the Lord spoke to me and told me that I was going to write a book based on Psalm 16, vs. 7-9.

I won't get into the details of the storyline of the book right now, but the gist of it is that at the time the Lord spoke to me and told me I would write that book, I was a struggling single mom, living in a single-wide trailer with my son. I was barely making ends meet! I was simply studying the Bible one day, when I suddenly heard the Lord speak to me about writing this book. He even showed me how to break the scripture up into chapters for the book! *YEARS BEFORE I WROTE IT!*

God sees your destiny, and will speak it over your life...no matter what your circumstances look like, He will cause your destiny to come to pass!

The fourth book, *Narco – Awake O Sleeper* was a product of a prophetic word I was hearing from the

Lord. I had been feeling in my spirit (and I still do!) that the church needs to WAKE UP out of its deep slumber. The Lord took me into some areas in which I felt that He wanted both the church body and me personally to come awake. These areas include hot-spots such as politics, relationship with God, unwrapping your giftings and Love.

Sometimes God gives me revelation or highlights a portion of His Word, and that is the inspiration to write. He also gave me an entire list of titles for books, to act as subject matter for them. He interjected this particular book, about how to write a book, in between "Narco" and the next one.

So just as all my ideas came from God, your ideas will come from Him also. It may not be as obvious as Him sending you on an undercover assignment to go to different denominational churches as He did with me in my first book, but it could be.

It could be your testimony, and in fact, should be your testimony! No one can take your testimony away from you, and no one can tell you it didn't happen! Your testimony is as individual as you are.

It could be an idea that the Lord has given to you by a prophetic word, an experience you had or one you want to research and know more about.

It could be your journal entries.

It could be a way to make money.

It could be a book to minister to a segment of the population, ie, young men or ex-drug addicts.

You may be able to tell people how you did something (and they can, too!) as in a DIY home repair guide.

It could be a "how-to" book, like this manual.

It could be a compilation of your blogs.

Whatever it is, the Lord has given it to you and He will see it through to fruition.

All you have to do is -- 1) Listen and 2) Write the book!

The second part is a lot tougher than it would seem, but you **must** press through the procrastination, the tiredness, the busyness, the "I-don't-feel-like-writing" and "the-grass-is-greener" syndrome.

Once you publish that first book it becomes addictive, in a good way, of course!

3. THE TITLE

The title of your book is EXTREMELY important! It is the hardest-working part of your literature!

Until you are a household name, like Stephen King or Joyce Meyers, the title to your book is tantamount to its success!

You want a title that will capture's a person's attention long enough for them to pick up the book and thumb through it. They will probably look at the back cover text next to see what the book is about, then the table of contents or simply thumb through the book -- but it's the TITLE that made them pick it up in the first place! So your title MUST grab their interest.

You want the title to explain the subject matter of the book, and make it sound interesting, too. You don't want to title your book *Daisies* if it's about ROSES!
Even if your book is about roses, that title is too general, non-descript and frankly, it's boring. Your title should be something more like *Growing Heritage Roses,* or *Caring for your Houston Rose Garden.*

If you are writing a book about your testimony, don't call it *My Testimony*. That is far too vague and nobody knows who YOU are (yet). If you started out as a drug addict and now you work with troubled teens, tie the two together, with something like, *From Drugs to Troubled Teens, and Everything In Between! -- How I bucked the death-grip of Meth, now I help teenagers do the same!*

I'm just shooting from the hip here, without any real thought or prayer beforehand. But you get the idea.

How-To's and DIY books are a lot easier, because they're pretty self-explanatory. However, coming from a marketing background, I would slant my book title toward the reader, who is always asking the question, "WIIFM...What's in it for me?" If someone sees a definite benefit in buying your book, if it is clear how it will help him or someone he loves, he will buy it. If it's all about YOU...well, no offense, but he may not be so interested.

People are always more interested in themselves than in you. It's just human nature. When you start a conversation with another person, you always say something like, "How are YOU?" You never walk up to someone and say, "I am GREAT!" Although that might be good for a laugh at a party, it won't sell many books.

This means that even for an autobiography, you want to write it in such a way that it will help the reader to overcome, to answer questions, learn a lesson, or somehow to do some other act that s/he needs to accomplish. And you need to start with the title.

So, let's go back to the drug-addict turned troubled-teen mentor example (not that I actually know anyone like that, at least consciously!) If Jane Doe wants to write a book about her life in order to help Janet Smith get out of the drug culture, specifically Methamphetamine, she might title it something like : *How I overcame the strongest addiction known to man, Meth – and you can, too!* If Jane Doe wants to help Janet Smith to get out of the drug culture and help her become a teen mentor to help teens do the same, she slants the book title in that direction ... *How I overcame drugs and now I help teenagers do the same!*

See, there will be Janet Smiths that will have an interest in both titles. It really depends on the author as to which group of readers s/he wants to write. Invariably

Jane will have readers from both groups pick up her book to read it. However, if it is titled toward one group specifically, she can market her book to that one class of people more easily, and that class of people will become more easily attracted to Jane's subject matter. It's symbiotic and helpful to both parties!

It is not always easy to write about something before knowing what the title will be. However, for me, each book was different, and it may be for you as well.

The title to my first book, *Spiritual Espionage, Going Undercover for the Kingdom of God!* was actually part of the story. When I finally realized what God was asking me to do – to go UNDERCOVER for Him -- I got so excited! I realized He was using me as a spiritual special agent that was going on assignment – Spiritual Espionage! I was going undercover for the Kingdom of God! Hence, that is how the book got its name.

I had the entire second book completely written before He gave me the title! I had absolutely no idea what the title to the book would be. It wasn't until I finally posed the question to God, after it was totally complete, and He started asking me about the book and its contents. Through a process of question and answer, I realized what He wanted to call it.

That is how the name for the book finally came to be.

Power Thieves – Seven Spirits that Steal Your Power and How to Get it Back! is EXACTLY what the book is about.

The title for the third book, *Spiritual Lightning Rods, connected to the Father of Lights* was again a part of the book. This time the title came organically through the writing of the words in one of the chapters. As I was writing, the phrase (which I'd never heard before, incidentally!) came to my mind, and it was ELECTRIFYING! I received such an incredible Holy Ghost witness as this statement flowed out my fingertips into the pages of the book, I just knew it had to be the title!

The next one was given to me before I sat down to write the book. I wrote the book to fulfill the title, *Narco – Awake O Sleeper*. God gave me the title to the book MONTHS before I sat down to write it (it's on my original list of book names!) and I had absolutely no idea what the book would (or should) be about.

As I sat down and listened to God speak, I wrote down the chapter headings first, and then wrote about each one. Again, God gave me every bit of the inspiration --- what to write, how to write it and what to call it. All I did was write down what He said.

Interestingly enough, now I know WHY all of my books have had such vastly different backgrounds, have been inspired in so many different ways and more....to help

YOU write YOUR book! Just as He sent the disciples out with baskets to pick up the bread crumbs, God wastes nothing! We are picking up the pieces and putting your book together, beginning now....!

4. WRITING THE BOOK ITSELF

I remember back in High School my English teacher would give us an assignment to "write an essay paper on such and such a subject." Since that was our directive, that is what we wrote about, and sometimes God still operates that way with me.

In elementary school we did book reports – little short books about books. In High school we had to think more independently, and come up with our own individual thoughts on a particular subject. In College there are term papers, Masters degrees require Thesis and Doctorates have dissertations! Each one is a version of a book, and many times Dissertations are published.

Depending on your level of formal education, you may already have written a book! You just haven't officially labeled it as such.

I have heard someone say that if you can write an email you can write a book. Yes, I agree. However, it takes virtually no effort to write an email, certainly no determination or commitment. If you can WRITE, you can WRITE a book! The only reason you have even gotten this far is because you have been given the unction to write a book. You WANT to. You just need someone to lay the groundwork for you, give you a track to run on. That is what I am attempting to do, by example.

How to write it comes from God. Sometimes God gives me the actual words. Other times I get a thought process, or as I am writing I suddenly realize that what I am writing about is *why* He made me go through a certain experience – just so that I can write about it and help somebody else, maybe even YOU!

As I indicated in the last part of the last chapter, He made me write 5-books 5-different ways, just so that YOU could have 5-Different Examples of how to sit down and write a book --- or 5!

Writing a book is not like writing music. There is no technical skill required, save for being able to string words together in a manner in which they can be understood well enough to pass along an idea.

Of course, you will want an editor to read your book and make corrections, spelling, grammatical and otherwise. If you are good in English, you can do it yourself. If you aren't...please hire somebody to do it!

You have heard that there is a "VOICE" to a particular author's way of writing. "I could actually hear her saying that as I read it!" That's what you want. You want to entertain AND inform. You want to carry the reader along on a wave of laughter, or leave him wringing his hands as he anxiously turns each page ensuring he follows your hero's journey all the way to the end.

You want to write like you speak. You speak a certain way, and that is the way you need to write. I don't mean "that theres and darned nears". I have read some literature that used that method of writing and, although F. Scott Fitzgerald pulled it off, it's hard to do.

That's not what I mean. What I mean is write about what you know, as **you know it**....not as you've heard it said. If you use colloquialisms when you speak, use them when you write. Don't TRY to use colloquialisms. It will appear contrived. If you know New England well, you can easily write about it, from your own perspective, as YOU know New England. Don't try to copy somebody else, or try to write from somebody else's perspective. It will not come off well.

And most importantly, don't plagiarize! You are you and you are an original. Be an original. Don't be a counterfeit. That is what the enemy wants. Be what God wants you to be, and that is the ONLY one of you that He made. There is none like you. Your experiences are original and your life is a one-of-a-kind.

Write about it.

5. EDITING

You wrote it, now read it. If it makes sense to you, it probably will to someone else, too. During the first edit, punctuation and grammar are not important. That comes later, through a second and third edit and thorough proof-reading.

I mentioned earlier that if you have mastered your native language, then you should feel confident to edit your own book. If you have a thought process, but don't really know how to write the book, including how to begin, what to say or even how to string words together you may want help from a third party. Preferably, this third party will actually write books, or at bare minimum edit them.

You don't need a master's degree in English to edit your book. You just need to have a firm grasp of sentence structure – subjects, objects, "run-on" sentences and the like. You will need to know when to use "I" and when to use "me" in a sentence. You will need to know how to put a topic in each paragraph.

I took English for years in the public school system. That is a topic that far exceeds the boundaries of this book title. However, if you need help, just ASK me. That is a small portion of what this book is for – to help YOU get your book written.

If the above has been a stumbling block for you, ASK me. I can help!! Edie@KingdomPromoters.org

A very good friend of mine writes books and sells them at his conferences. Some of his books have typographical errors in them, spelling errors and sometimes formatting errors. They are not terrible, and it doesn't matter – his books still sell! More importantly, the people that read them love both the books and HIM!

See, I understand there is a spirit of EXCELLENCE to which we want to adhere, but understand this --- ultimately, most people won't KNOW that you have not used a proper verb tense, that there is a dangling participle, or you have misspelled "Pseudonym". If you do a good, solid job of editing your book/s and you find a typo later after it goes to print, it is NOT the end of the world! Just correct the typo for the next printing run.

Here is my recommended course to write your book and edit it:

1. Write down your thoughts and just GO. Don't get very deep in detail, because you will get hung up. I REPEAT --- DO NOT GET HUNG UP IN THE DETAILS. Just write, making something akin to an outline (or an actual outline if you need one). Then fill in the gaps and details as a second and/or third step.

2. Once you go through your book and fill in the details, then separate it into chapters, or into similar subjects. Each book topic will lend itself to a certain way of categorizing the information contained within it. If you are publishing your blogs, you may wish to avoid publishing the dates the entries were posted to your blog – this will quickly DATE your book and make it obsolete. Just break it up into chapters....if you have 23 posts in your blog, simply make 23 chapters! Or, if three or four of your blogs have similar subject matter, then group them together and make that a chapter. That is up to you.

3. Now comes the tedious but necessary part. Once you are satisfied with the CONTENT of your book, you will need to edit it. This is where you go through your book line by line, looking for "run-on" sentences, sentence fragments, misspelled words and typographical errors. You are also looking for incomplete thought processes, redundancies in thoughts (or actual words), and any kind of error of any type! I know that's pretty broad, but that's the truth.

4. Utilize the spell-checker feature of your computer word processing program. It also has a grammar correcting feature as well; however, it is NOT infallible. Your computer program may not be able to distinguish between "WOULD" and "WOOD". You will need to manually correct it. Some of these errors are extremely hard to catch, but this is your job as the editor. The one that really bugs me the most is "your" (possessive) and "you're" (you are). But that's just me! Computers do not catch this error, and frankly, most people don't either. So, if you find one or two of these, don't worry about it. It's not the end of the world. It's just a typo.

5. Please don't fall in love with your prose. Your job as the editor is TO EDIT. Back in the pre-digital movie days, filmmakers used actual, physical film.

They had reels and reels of the stuff from shooting hours and hours and hours of footage. Have you ever seen how they used to edit all those dozens of hours of raw footage into a 90-minute movie? They literally CUT IT....with SCISSORS!   Parts of the actual physical movie ended up on the floor! You may actually find yourself re-writing or even cutting chunks out of your document. You may end up scrapping the entire project! You may get into it and decide that you really don't WANT to write about this particular topic! Or that you need to do more research first. It may be too controversial, or just not interesting. Of course, if YOU are interested in the topic you can be sure that others are as well. No matter what, the bottom line is this --- as the editor your job is to be sure the book is properly edited, whatever that takes.

6. A word of warning: Watch out for Slander. Change names to protect the innocent. And if you want your family to read your books, don't write stories about them and include them in your books! I learned the hard way that what I thought was an amusing anecdote actually hurt (offended) another family member. I was very saddened by their spin on what I had written, but honestly, I should have asked them if I could include that

story in my book. They would have said, "NO!" and I would have deleted it out of my Word doc. They probably would still be speaking to me today. So, PLEASE --- get permission to write a story about anyone in your family. It's wisdom. And if they say, "NO!" – don't do it. No matter how funny the story is, how relevant, how compelling. It's not worth it.

7. If you include ANYTHING that is written by anyone else, get permission to use it in your book. You absolutely MUST have permission from the author in writing. If they say, "NO!" delete it out of your document and find another way of saying it.

8. If you share a story about another person, make sure you get their permission to use it, especially if that person is well-known or their story would add credibility to your topic.

9. Always get WRITTEN PERMISSION and keep it on file. I haven't run into this yet, but I have had some experience with working with well known ministry personalities, and it's a rule for us.

I was just reminded of a story. Years ago I was a licensed dog-groomer in Arizona. I was grooming a cocker spaniel one day, working on him, and working on him. I guess I had spent too long and had tried too hard to get the dog's clip PERFECT, because the owner of the dog grooming salon came up to me. She looked at me and said, "Edie, there comes a time when a dog is "DONE". This dog is done. Now put him in his kennel."

There will come a time when YOUR dog is done! You will need to see that and put the dog in his kennel to await his owner to come and pick him up.

What I mean by that is that there will come a time when your book is done. Don't over-think it, don't over write it and don't over-edit it! Remember what I said about my friend and his books with the typos that still sell anyway in spite of them!

You will NEVER know everything there is to know about a particular subject, so write what you DO know! You will never be a perfect speller, so do the best you can. You will never have a perfect book so don't even try!

Each book is a piece of art. It is NOT a science. Your book is uniquely crafted, a part of and an extension of YOU. No one can write about the subject that you have chosen quite the same way that you can with your unique perspective. Some are better. A LOT are worse! And sadly, most not at all.

Don't let anything stop you from getting your book into print.

6. YOUR BOOK COVER

The Cover Art

Once your book is thoroughly edited, you will want to design the cover for it. There are lots of ways to do this. How you do it is up to you. You may be able to use a template available from an online source. You may want an artist to create an original work of art to use as the backdrop for your book cover. You may want a photographer to take your picture (or any picture) to use on the cover or on the back of the book. What you do is up to you. How you do it adheres to rigorous industry standards!

There are many terms used in cover art that are NOT in general use. Terms such as "bleed", "camera-ready",

"CMYK", "tic-marks" and the like simply do not exist in every day conversation, unless you work on book covers for a living. It is knowing WHAT these terms mean, and how they apply to your cover art that matters. That is beyond the scope of this text, so I will leave it up to the professionals.

Allow it to suffice that even if you are an amazing photographer or artist, it still takes someone with an extensive knowledge of publishing industry standards to get your product out with a professional looking cover.

WHAT you put on your cover is entirely up to you. All of mine are different. One is a photograph I took on a road trip to preach in South Dakota. Another is a .jpg I found online. Another is a picture I found elsewhere.

I try to make them all "speak" about the subject matter. *Spiritual Espionage* is a black and white chessboard with rain on it, which speaks about Holy Spirit and the strategy of what God was doing sending me undercover.

Spiritual Lightning Rods cover is a cityscape of tall buildings at night that have lightning rods with bolts of lightning actually hitting them. This one needs little interpretation!

Narco, Awake O Sleeper is a coffee cup full of coffee beans, some of which have spilled out all over the table.

Everyone thinks of caffeine when they think of coffee and coffee speaks about "waking up".

Each of them "speaks" to the subject of the book. It was intentional.

However, you can do whatever you want. It is a popular tactic to put the author's photograph on the front of the book, and I may do that someday when I get a professional portrait taken. Currently I only use photographs on the backs of my books, for the "author photo" section.

Back Cover Text

The most difficult part of writing the entire book in my opinion is the back cover text, or "blurb", which is a funny word in itself. It is difficult for me to condense an entire book into a few lines, and make it interesting enough for someone to want to take it home with them! This is the point of the back cover text, to "sell" your book to the reader, and make them want to read more.

What I have done to date (and this is not necessarily THE only way to do it) is to pick a sentence or sentences that are in the book itself that touch on the subject matter of the book, explain some of what I am trying to accomplish (or do for the reader), but do not give away "the punch line" and use that as my blurb.

The second hardest part of the process for me is to write the copy that will be distributed online to the various book seller websites, i.e., Amazon, Kindle etc. This is almost as difficult in my opinion, and definitely more tedious, than even the blurb. However, there are methods to consider depending on which genre of book you are writing, whether it's a novel or a non-fiction book. I'll discuss this in greater detail at a future point, at a book-writing class. For now, let it suffice to say that you want to expand on the back cover text to about 2 paragraphs and make it interesting enough for someone to pick your book from dozens of other online titles!

However, once you have done it, it's done. So just grab the elephant and take a bite. Keep going and take another bite. Pretty soon you'll be done and moving onto the part of the process that you like...the writing of your next book.

7. MARKETING

The last and final stage of the life of your new book is getting it into the eager hands of those who would like to read it. You will do this by MARKETING your book.

If you are blessed, your book will be picked up by a major publishing house and you will never have to do this part. If not you will become extremely familiar with Kindle, Amazon, Facebook, Twitter, and all the other similar methods of getting your book "out there".

I read recently that you must know HOW you are going to market your book before you ever write it! I do not totally agree with this statement, although I knew how I would market my books before I began to write them. In fact, I wrote them FOR this purpose, so I guess the statement is relevant.

In my opinion, you have a book in you --- so write it! Whether ANYONE ever reads it or not, write your book! Whether it's a best-seller or it sells just a few copies, write your book. If you give it away to family members, they will never forget it, because every single one of them has WANTED to write a book, but just never "got around to it". They'll be envious, too! All of them will look at you with awe, and wonder how their little brother (aunt, cousin, sister, etc.) found the time and the audacity to BELIEVE s/he could write a book, do it, and publish it!

If you are serious about selling your books, then submit to a true publishing house, one that has a publicist and an editor, will do your cover art and keep your book on the right path.

If you are serious about getting your opinion out there, set up conferences and sell your books. Attorneys hold conferences to do it all the time. So do real estate agents, and you can too!

If you do not want to be a speaker at a conference, let other speakers sell your books for you! All speakers are happy to have books on their table. It's hard and time consuming to be both a speaker and an author, although obviously not impossible. However, any time you allow a third party to sell your books for you, be aware that you will need to discount the price, and sell them "wholesale" to that third party. They will then sell it at "retail".

The bottom line is this: if you sell the books, you keep all the profits. However, if you are unable or unwilling to "sell" your books to the end consumer, you can still sell books....you will just make less money doing it.

 Sometimes it is better to just get your book "out there", if that is your goal. One of my author friends says his books are giant business cards, and he would rather they be out doing something than sitting on his shelf. I agree!

So, don't let marketing your book become an obstacle. Just find a friendly publisher, or a friendly speaker who needs books for his or her book table. It will be no time at all before you are selling out on all your titles!

8. HELP

For Help with Publishing and More Assistance:

If you need assistance with writing, editing or publishing your book, or you just don't know where to begin, contact me:

Edie Bayer,

Edie@KingdomPromoters.org

Website:

http://www.KingdomPromoters.org

I can help you get your book from conception to published to marketed to sold! Contact me today.

ABOUT THE AUTHOR

Edie Bayer's primary focus is to promote and advance the Kingdom of God by helping people to hear and recognize the voice of the Lord, and then act upon it. Edie has served with international ministers Joan Hunter and Paulette Reed as well as Darren Canning and Dr. Judy Laird. Edie ministers as a Preacher and Prophet of God. She is an author, a speaker and itinerant minister.

Edie and her husband Darryl formed Kingdom Promoters (www.KingdomPromoters.org), to help further God's Kingdom by acting as an incubator to assist fledgling ministries in their start-up stages. Kingdom Promoters also hosts itinerant speakers and travelling ministers such as Dr. Linda Smith and Apostle William Dillon, as well as author Carol Sewell, among others.

You may reach Edie and Darryl at their websites, www.KingdomPromoters.org and www.TexasBrass.com

Darryl Bayer has many CD's available on CDBaby.com and Amazon.com. You can find videos of them on YouTube.com

You may also read and sign up for Edie's blog, http://ediebear1.wordpress.com .

You may also wish to email Edie, Edie@KingdomPromoters.org

Darryl and Edie are available to play, preach and prophesy at your church, ladies group or other event.

Edie also conducts "Write that Book" conferences.

Contact us!

Other titles by Edie Bayer:
1.   *Spiritual Espionage, Going Undercover for the Kingdom of God,* ©2014, ISBN: 9780615985510
2.   *Power Thieves, 7-Spirits that Steal Your Power and How to Get it Back!* © 2014, ISBN: 9780692211151
3.   *Spiritual Lightning Rods, Connected to the Father of Lights,* © 2014, ISBN: 9780692228036
4.   *Narco, Awake O Sleeper,* ©2014, ISBN: 9780692330005
5.   Write that Book! You have a Book in You – Now Write it! © 2015, ISBN: 0692350756

Watch for new book and music releases coming soon!

Edie and Darryl reside on a small homestead north of the Houston area. They raise chickens, ducks, quail and rabbits and have three cats. Edie has two children and three grandchildren.